1 MONTH OF FREE READING

at

www.ForgottenBooks.com

By purchasing this book you are eligible for one month membership to ForgottenBooks.com, giving you unlimited access to our entire collection of over 700,000 titles via our web site and mobile apps.

To claim your free month visit:
www.forgottenbooks.com/free1121441

* Offer is valid for 45 days from date of purchase. Terms and conditions apply.

ISBN 978-0-331-42063-0
PIBN 11121441

This book is a reproduction of an important historical work. Forgotten Books uses state-of-the-art technology to digitally reconstruct the work, preserving the original format whilst repairing imperfections present in the aged copy. In rare cases, an imperfection in the original, such as a blemish or missing page, may be replicated in our edition. We do, however, repair the vast majority of imperfections successfully; any imperfections that remain are intentionally left to preserve the state of such historical works.

Forgotten Books is a registered trademark of FB &c Ltd.
Copyright © 2017 FB &c Ltd.
FB &c Ltd, Dalton House, 60 Windsor Avenue, London, SW19 2RR.
Company number 08720141. Registered in England and Wales.

For support please visit www.forgottenbooks.com

AVERY ARCHITECTURAL AND FINE ARTS LIBRARY

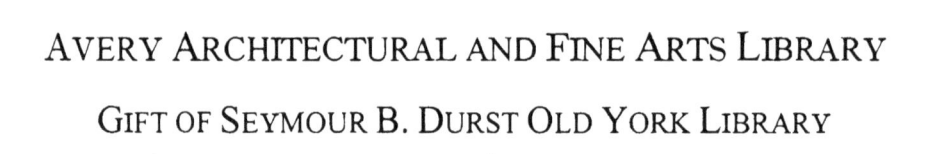

GIFT OF SEYMOUR B. DURST OLD YORK LIBRARY

2.5 POLXL
POL 4C

Certificate of Incorporation

Constitution

Rules

and

List of Members

of **The**

Democratic Club

of the

City of New York

Club-House:
617 Fifth Avenue

1892

offsite
JK
2319
NE
Dublin
N.Y.

DOUGLAS TAYL
8 WARREN ST
NEW YORK

OFFICERS
1892

PRESIDENT, - - - JOHN H. V. ARNOLD
VICE-PRESIDENT, - - - BARTOW S. WEEKS
TREASURER, - - - J. ROCKWELL FAY
SECRETARY, - - - - - W. E. CURTIS

BOARD OF GOVERNORS

TERM EXPIRES DECEMBER, 1892

JOHN H. V. ARNOLD   J. ROCKWELL FAY
BARTOW S. WEEKS   W. E. CURTIS
Ex-officio

HENRY A. GILDERSLEEVE   J. MAXWELL LUMMIS
JOSEPH F. MOSHER   E. D. NEUSTADT

TERM EXPIRES DECEMBER, 1893

ORLANDO B. POTTER   A. WALKER OTIS
GILBERT D. LAMB   HAMILTON B. TOMPKINS

TERM EXPIRES DECEMBER, 1894

JEFFERSON M. LEVY   THOMAS E. CRIMMINS
ROGER FOSTER   EDWARD F. O'DWYER

HOUSE COMMITTEE

JEFFERSON M. LEVY, *Chairman.*

ROGER FOSTER   GEO. TRIMBLE DAVIDSON
THOMAS E. CRIMMINS   JAMES J. TRAYNOR

CERTIFICATE OF INCORPORATION

State of New York,
City and County of New York, } ss.:

We, John H. V. Arnold, President, Jefferson M. Levy, Vice-President, William E. Curtis, Secretary, G. Willett Van Nest, Corresponding Secretary, J. Rockwell Fay, Treasurer, and Bartow S. Weeks, Chairman of Executive Committee, being officers and members of an unincorporated political club in the City of New York, known by the name or title of The Democratic Club of the City of New York, and being of full age, and citizens of the United States, and citizens of the State of New York, do hereby certify that we desire, on behalf of said Club, having been thereto duly authorized by vote of said Club, to avail ourselves of the provisions of an act of the Legislature of this State, entitled "An Act for the Incorporation of Political Clubs," passed April 29th, 1886.

That this certificate is signed, acknowledged and filed under the provisions of said act authorizing the incorporation of existing unincorporated political clubs.

That the name or title by which such Club shall be known in law is "THE DEMOCRATIC CLUB OF THE CITY OF NEW YORK."

The particular business and object of such Club is to foster and disseminate Democratic principles.

That the number of the Executive Committee managing the affairs of said Club is twenty-five.

The names of said Committee for the first year are as follows:

JOHN H. V. ARNOLD,	ARTHUR M. JACOBUS,
WILLIAM E. CURTIS,	JOHN BROOKS LEAVITT,
G. WILLETT VAN NEST,	J. MAXWELL LUMMIS,
J. ROCKWELL FAY,	STEPHEN MCCORMICK,
BARTOW S. WEEKS,	ROBERT G. MONROE,
E. ELLERY ANDERSON,	WILLIAM H. O'DWYER,
HANS S. BEATTIE,	A. WALKER OTIS,
F. KINGSBURY CURTIS,	LUCIEN OUDIN,
ALFRED J. DICKERSON,	PERCIVAL J. PARRIS,
ROGER FOSTER,	JAMES H. SKIDMORE,
HENRY GREENFIELD,	P. T. WALL,
THOMAS HARLAND,	EDWARD B. WHITNEY,

OSCAR YENNI.

CERTIFICATE OF INCORPORATION

In Witness Whereof, we have hereunto set our hands this eighth day of August, in the year one thousand eight hundred and ninety.

John H. V. Arnold,
Jefferson M. Levy,
William E. Curtis,
G. Willett Van Nest,
J. Rockwell Fay,
Bartow S. Weeks.

State, City and County of New York, ss.:

On this eighth day of August, in the year one thousand eight hundred and ninety, before me personally came and appeared John H. V. Arnold, Jefferson M. Levy, William E. Curtis, G. Willett Van Nest, J. Rockwell Fay and Bartow S. Weeks, to me severally known, and known to me to be the individuals described in, and who executed the foregoing instrument, and severally acknowledged to me that they executed the same.

LeRoy Porter,
Commissioner of Deeds, New York City.

CERTIFICATE OF INCORPORATION

State of New York, }
Office of the Secretary of State, } ss.:

I have compared the preceding with the original Certificate of Incorporation of "The Democratic Club of the City of New York," with acknowledgment thereto annexed, filed and recorded in this office on the 14th day of August, 1890, and do 𝕳𝖊𝖗𝖊𝖇𝖞 𝕮𝖊𝖗𝖙𝖎𝖋𝖞 the same to be a correct transcript therefrom and of the whole of said original.

(SEAL) 𝖂𝖎𝖙𝖓𝖊𝖘𝖘 my hand and the Seal of office of the Secretary of State at the City of Albany, this 14th day of August, one thousand eight hundred and ninety.

Frank Rice,
Secretary of State.

CERTIFICATE OF INCORPORATION

State of New York, } ss.:
City and County of New York,

I, Edward F. Reilly, Clerk of the said City and County, and Clerk of the Supreme Court of said State for said County, **Do hereby Certify** that the

CERTIFICATE OF INCORPORATION
OF
The Democratic Club of the City of New York,

with acknowledgment thereto annexed, was filed and recorded in this office on the eighteenth day of August, 1890.

In Witness Whereof, I have hereunto subscribed my name and affixed (SEAL) my official seal this 18th day of August, 1890.

Edward F. Reilly,
Clerk.

CONSTITUTION

ARTICLE I.

ORGANIZATION AND OBJECT

1. This Club is a corporation incorporated under the laws of the State of New York, by the name THE DEMOCRATIC CLUB OF THE CITY OF NEW YORK.

2. Its object is to foster, disseminate and give effect to Democratic principles.

3. Its participation as an organization in elections or in the endorsement of candidates for office, shall be confined to National and State canvasses.

ARTICLE II.

MEMBERSHIP

1. The number of members, exclusive of non-resident members, shall not exceed one thousand. All members who are not non-resident or honorary members shall be embraced in the term "resident members" where hereinafter used.

2. All persons who were resident, non-resi-

dent or honorary members of the unincorporated organization known as The Young Men's Democratic Club of the City of New York, at the time its name was changed to The Democratic Club of the City of New York, and who have not since died or resigned from the membership of the last-named Club, and all persons who have since the change aforesaid been elected resident or non-resident members of said last-named Club, and have duly qualified as such, are hereby declared to be resident, non-resident and honorary members respectively of The Democratic Club of the City of New York, which shall hereafter consist of such persons, and such others as may hereafter be elected and qualify as members of said Club under the provisions of this Constitution.

3. Any male adult citizen of the United States who shall be in sympathy with the objects of this Club, may become a resident member upon election by the Board of Governors, and payment of the initiation fee and dues hereinafter prescribed for resident members.

4. Any male adult citizen of the United States, not residing within the City of New York, may become a non-resident member upon election as such by the Board of Governors, and payment of the initiation fee and dues hereinafter prescribed for non-resident members. Non-resident members, to the number of 500, may be elected between February 1st, 1891, and January 1st, 1893, who shall not be required to pay any initiation fee, provided members so elected shall reside at a distance not iess than 25 miles from the City of New York.

5. If payment of initiation fee and dues is not made within sixty days after notice of election shall have been given to the person so elected, or to his proposer or seconder, the election shall be void.

6. Non-resident members shall have all the rights and privileges of resident members, except that they cannot vote or hold office in the Club. They shall be subject to the same liabilities and penalties as resident members, but such exemption on the part of any non-resident member shall cease and he shall be-

come a resident member whenever he shall become a resident of the City of New York. A non-resident member, upon becoming a resident member, shall be liable for the dues of the half year then current at the rate prescribed for resident members, but shall be credited on account thereof with whatever sum he shall have paid on account of his dues as non-resident member for the current year. Any non-resident may become a resident member upon the same terms, and upon giving notice to the Secretary that he desires to become such resident member. Any resident member not indebted to the Club, who is or becomes a non-resident within the meaning of this section, may, upon his request, be made a non-resident member by a vote of the Board of Governors; but no reduction in his dues by reason of such non-residence shall be made during the then current half year. No non-resident member shall, however, become a resident member until he shall have paid the difference between the initiation fee of a non-resident and that of a resident member as hereinafter prescribed.

7. Candidates for membership must be proposed by one member and seconded by another, in writing, in a book kept for that purpose, and notice thereof sent to the resident members of the Club, at least ten days previous to the meeting of the Board of Governors at which they are balloted for, and their names must be posted in the Club-House for the same length of time, in the place provided for posting such notices.

8. On the death, resignation or expulsion of a member, all his rights and interests in the Club and its property shall wholly cease and determine, but he shall not thereby be released from any liability to the Club for any dues, assessments, or other indebtedness which may have accrued before he ceased to be a member.

9. Any member wishing to resign shall send his resignation in writing to the Secretary. No member can resign while indebted to the Club.

CONSTITUTION

ARTICLE III.

MEETINGS OF THE CLUB

1. There shall be an annual meeting of the Club for the election of officers and Governors, and such other business as may come before it, on the first Monday in December in each year, at eight o'clock P. M., notice of which meeting shall be mailed to every member ten days before the date of such meeting. If no quorum be present at the annual meeting, the presiding officer may adjourn such meeting for not less than one week, nor more than two weeks therefrom, at which adjourned meeting the same business may be transacted as might have been transacted at the annual meeting, and with the like effect as if transacted thereat, but notice of such adjourned meeting shall be mailed to members at least five days before the same shall be held. Special meetings of the Club shall be held whenever the Board of Governors shall deem the same necessary, or whenever at least twenty-five voting members of the Club shall present

to the President a written request for the same, specifying the object of the meeting, in which case no other business than that specified in the notice shall be transacted at that meeting. Notices of all special meetings shall be mailed to each member at least three days before the same shall be held.

2. All meetings of the Club shall be held at the Club-House.

ARTICLE IV.

OFFICERS

The officers of the Club shall be a President, Vice-President, Secretary, Treasurer and twelve Governors, which officers and Governors shall together constitute the Board of Governors, the said officers being *ex-officio* members of such Board.

ARTICLE V.

ELECTION OF OFFICERS

1. The President, Vice-President, Secretary and Treasurer shall be elected at the annual

meeting in each year, unless a quorum shall not be present, in which case they shall be elected at the adjourned annual meeting. The remaining twelve members of the Board of Governors shall be elected at the annual meeting on the first Monday of December, 1890, or, if a quorum be not present, at the adjourned annual meeting in said year. Four thereof shall be elected to serve for one year from said first Monday of December, 1890, four to serve for two years from said date, and four to serve for three years from said date. Thereafter, at each annual meeting or adjourned annual meeting, four members of said Board of Governors shall be elected, who shall hold office for three years from the first Monday of December in the year of their election.

2. All elections shall be by ballot, and all officers and Governors shall hold office until their successors shall be elected.

3. Twenty-five voting members shall constitute a quorum for the transaction of business at any meeting of the Club.

4. There shall be mailed to each member,

except non-resident members, at least ten days before the annual meeting, a statement of the members nominated for officers and Governors, provided such nominations are in writing, signed by not less than ten voting members of the Club, and shall have been handed to the Secretary at least fifteen days before such annual meeting, and it shall be the duty of the Secretary to post all such nominations in the place provided for such purpose in the Club-House, and keep the same so posted during the ten days preceding the annual meeting at which such nominations are to be acted upon. At the opening of each annual meeting or adjourned annual meeting, the presiding officer shall appoint three members of the Club as tellers to receive and canvass the votes, and thereupon the poll shall be opened, and be kept open for two hours. The tellers shall receive the ballots of the members, who must vote in person, and on the completion of the canvass they shall certify the result to the presiding officer. The nominees who shall have the highest number of votes for the respective offices for which they are nominated shall be declared elected.

5. Non-resident and honorary members are ineligible to hold office in the Club, and no member shall be entitled to vote or hold office who is in arrears for dues.

ARTICLE VI.

BOARD OF GOVERNORS

1. The government and management of the Club shall be confided to the Board of Governors, to be constituted and elected as hereinabove provided. They shall have power to fill any vacancy in their number until the next annual meeting of the Club, or adjourned annual meeting of the Club, succeeding the happening of such vacancy.

2. Any member of the Board of Governors, other than *ex-officio* members, who shall absent himself from three consecutive regular meetings of the Board, unless he shall have previously obtained permission so to do from the Board, or shall present at the next regu-

lar meeting an excuse for his absence, satisfactory to the members of the Board present, shall be deemed to have resigned, and his office as Governor shall thereupon become vacant.

3. The Board of Governors shall have power to appoint (and at any time remove and replace the same or any member or members thereof) a House Committee, to be composed of not less than three members of the Club, any of whom may or may not be members of said Board of Governors, the duty of which Committee shall be, subject to the direction and control of the Board of Governors, to direct and manage the affairs of the Club-House and to receive and act upon complaints and suggestions of members, reporting monthly, or oftener if required, to the Board. Said Committee shall have the general charge of said Club-House and its servants, with authority to expend such sums in respect to the same as may be voted therefor by the Board of Governors. If at any time the indebtedness of any member of the Club upon the books of the House

Committee shall amount to twenty-five dollars, such member shall receive no further credit until such indebtedness has been paid and the House Committee shall notify him to that effect. If the accounts of the House Committee on the first of any month shall show an indebtedness to the Club on the part of any member, it shall be the duty of the House Committee to render to him a bill thereof, and such member shall be required to pay the same within ten days thereafter. The name of any member failing to pay his indebtedness within ten days after the bill thereof shall have been rendered to him as above provided shall be conspicuously posted in the Club-House at the expiration of said ten days, and notice thereof mailed to such member by the House Committee. The name of any member in arrears, and who shall have failed for the space of five days after such posting to pay his said indebtedness, shall be reported by the House Committee to the Board of Governors at the next meeting of the latter thereafter. Such member may thereupon by vote of such Board be suspended from the privileges of the Club-House for such time as the said Board shall specify, and it shall also have power whenever it shall see fit, to fix by vote and notify such member of a limit of time within which he shall be required to pay such indebtedness or subject himself in default thereof to be dropped from the roll of membership, and any such member who shall fail to pay his said indebtedness within the time so limited after being notified as above provided shall be deemed to have withdrawn from the Club and his name may be dropped from the roll thereof by the vote of such Board.

4. The Board of Governors shall also have power to prescribe rules for the admission of strangers; to make rules for the use of the Club-House by the members, and for their conduct in the Club-House; to fix penalties for violation of the rules, and to enforce or remit the same; to call special meetings of the Club to consider any specific subject or subjects; to make rules for their own government, and to fix and enforce penalties for the violation of such rules; to appoint such sub-

committees from time to time as it may deem advisable, which sub-committees may be appointed wholly or partly from members of the Club who shall not be members of the Board of Governors, as such Board shall deem advisable.

5. Said Board of Governors shall also have power to censure, suspend, drop or expel any member for a violation of the Constitution or a rule, or for any conduct not in violation of the Constitution or a rule which, in the opinion of such Board, is improper and prejudicial to the welfare or reputation of the Club; but no member shall be censured, suspended or expelled unless by the affirmative vote by ballot of two-thirds of all the Governors, nor without written notice of the charge against him and of the time when he can submit to the Board a written answer to such charge. Any member censured or expelled by the Board of Governors, may, within five days after the mailing to him of notice of such action, appeal therefrom to the Club, and such appeal shall be heard at the next meeting of the Club, occurring not less than ten days

after such appeal has been taken, and notice thereof shall be given to every member with the notice of such meeting.

6. All elections of resident and non-resident members of the Club shall be by the Board of Governors, and by ballot, three adverse ballots excluding, and all votes, conversations and debates in the Board on the admission of a candidate, or on the censure, suspension or expulsion of a member, shall be held by the Governors in secrecy.

7. A vote upon the admission of a proposed member, or upon the censure, suspension or expulsion of a member shall, on the motion of any Governor, be reconsidered at the same meeting at which said vote was passed, and a second ballot shall be taken; but no such vote can be reconsidered, modified or rescinded at any subsequent meeting unless notice in writing shall have been sent to each Governor at least ten days before the meeting that such vote will be then brought up for reconsideration.

8. A candidate rejected at one meeting shall not, within six months thereafter, be

again balloted for. Candidates whose names shall have been laid over at two successive meetings shall not be balloted for until the candidates whose names succeeded theirs on the list shall have been elected or rejected.

9. The Board of Governors shall meet once a month, except during the months of July and August; but special meetings of the Board may be called on two days' notice by order of the President, Vice-President, or the House Committee. At least seven members of the Board shall be present to constitute a quorum at any of its meetings.

ARTICLE VII.

DUTIES OF OFFICERS

1. The President, or, in his absence, the Vice-President, shall preside at all meetings of the Club and of the Board of Governors, but in their absence a meeting of the Club or of the Board of Governors may elect a presiding officer for such meeting.

2. The Treasurer shall keep the accounts of the Club and report thereon monthly to

the Board of Governors, and the Secretary shall keep the records of the Club. The officers shall also have such other powers and duties as may from time to time be prescribed by the Club or by the Board of Governors.

3. At each annual meeting of the Club the Board of Governors shall, through the Treasurer, make a report to the Club of the financial condition of the Club, with such other particulars in respect to the condition or needs of the Club as such Board may consider necessary. Such report shall be prepared and printed, and a copy thereof sent to each resident member of the Club, with the notice of the annual meeting.

ARTICLE VIII.

FEES AND DUES

The initiation fee for resident members shall be twenty-five dollars, and for non-resident members fifteen dollars. The half-yearly dues of resident members shall be twelve dollars and fifty cents, payable in advance on the first day of January and July in each year. The dues of non-resident members shall be ten dollars, payable annually on the first day of January in each year.

ARTICLE IX.

PENALTIES

Any member who shall fail to pay his dues for two months, after the same shall become payable as herein prescribed, in any year, shall cease to be a member, without any action of the Club or of the Board of Governors, but said Board may, in its discretion, at any time within ten months thereafter, reinstate such member upon his paying all his arrears of dues and other indebtedness to the Club.

ARTICLE X.

NOTICES

A member may inscribe in a book, to be kept for that purpose, a mail address for notices, and he shall be held to have received any notice when it has been mailed to that address. In the absence of such inscription, any notice may, with like effect, be deposited in the post office, addressed as the Secretary may think most likely to insure its prompt delivery.

ARTICLE XI.

MONTHLY MEETINGS OF THE CLUB

There shall be a Monthly Meeting of the Club on the third Monday of each month, except during the months of July and August, for the transaction of such business as may come before it, and four days' notice, in writing, of such Monthly Meeting shall be mailed to each member.

ARTICLE XII.

AMENDMENTS TO THE CONSTITUTION

Amendments to the Constitution may be made at any annual meeting of the Club, or at any special meeting called for that purpose by a two-thirds vote in the affirmative, a quorum being present and voting; but no amendment shall be acted on at any meeting unless proposed by the Board of Governors or by a member of the Club, and notice thereof, in writing, given to the Secretary at least fifteen days before the meeting, and the Secretary shall post a copy of such proposed amendment in the Club-House for not less than ten days before such meeting, and shall send by mail to each member of the Club a copy thereof not less than five days before such meeting.

ARTICLE XIII.

The officers in office at the time of the adoption of this Constitution shall continue as such until the officers elected at the first election hereunder shall assume their respective offices.

RULES

FOR THE ADMISSION OF VISITORS.

THE privileges of the Club-House for the period of two weeks, upon the application of a member, may be extended to any person not residing within the City; but no person shall be allowed such privilege oftener than once in three months.

Any visitor accompanying a member shall be entitled to admission to all parts of the Club-House except the Card Rooms.

Members shall be responsible for the indebtedness incurred by any visitor introduced by them.

HOUSE RULES

1. The Club-House shall be opened at seven o'clock A. M. Admittance cannot be claimed after one o'clock A. M.

2. No liquors will be served in the Reception Room or Library at any hour, and none in the front parlor before six P. M.

3. Meals for fewer than four persons cannot be served in the private dining-room.

HOUSE RULES

4. Members will be charged for their rooms until notice is given at the office of their desire to vacate them.

5. Members on leaving their rooms are requested to lock the door and leave the key in the office.

6. The Club will not be responsible for property left in the rooms.

7. Pipe smoking is not permitted in any part of the House.

8. Smoking is prohibited in the dining-room.

9. Dogs will not be allowed in the Club-House.

10. Publications belonging to the Club must not be taken from the Club-House.

11. Members shall not give any fee or gratuity to a servant of the Club.

12. Complaints of any inefficiency in the management or service of the Club must be made, in writing, to the House Committee, in the book furnished for the purpose.

13. Complaints of over-charges or errors in accounts must be made to the Steward.

HONORARY MEMBERS

Grover Cleveland.................. 15 Broad Street.

RESIDENT MEMBERS

A

ABNEY, JOHN R. . . . . 80 Broadway
ACKERT, ALFRED T. 37 Wall Street
ACKLEY, J. EDWARD . . . . 35 Wall Street
ADAMS, JOHN J. . . . . 110 West 74th Street
ADAMS, JOHN QUINCY. . . . . 79 West 91st Street
ADAMS, FRED. T. . . . . 102 Broadway
ALEXANDER, CHARLES B. . . . . 120 Broadway
ALLEN, HENRY. 11 East 43d Street
ALLEN, CHARLES F. . . . . 153 West 45th Street
ALLEN, FREDERICK H. . . . . 36 Wall Street
ALLING, A. A. . . . . 15 Broad Street
ALLING, R. B. . . . . 187 Greenwich Street
ANDERSON, E. ELLERY. . . . . 10 Wall Street
ANDREWS, W. S. . . . . 101 East 89th Street
ARMSTRONG, DR. S. T. . . . . 166 West 54th Street
ANDREWS, H. F. . . . . 261 Broadway
ARNOLD, REGINALD HARVEY. . . . . 206 Broadway
ARNOLD, OSCAR M. . . . . 14 White Street
ARNOLD, JOHN H. V. . . . . 206 Broadway
ARONSON, ALBERT. . . . . 39th Street and Broadway
ARROWSMITH, WILLIAM. . . . . 229 Broadway

RESIDENT MEMBERS

AUERBACH, JOSEPH S.................3 Broad Street
AUSTEN, DAVID E.... ....280 Broadway
AUTENRIETH, HENRY G...............320 Broadway

B

BAGE, ALFRED C....................22 Warren Street
BAKER, ALFRED J...................115 Broadway
BALDWIN, CHRISTOPHER C............11 Wall Street
BARKER, RICHARD H................32 Liberty Street
BARNARD, HORACE...................102 Broadway
BARRY, THOMAS G...................120 Broadway
BARTLETT, FRANKLIN.................41 Park Row
BAYAUD, GEORGE D..................62 New Street
BEALL, JOHN A.....................149 Broadway
BEATTIE, HANS S...................120 Broadway
BECKETT, CHARLES H................160 Broadway
BEEKMAN, HENRY R............119 East 18th Street
BELL, THOMAS O...............157 Chambers Street
BELMONT, AUGUST...................23 Nassau Street
BELMONT, PERRY....................23 Nassau Street
BERRY, ARTHUR.....................200 Broadway
BEYER, S. D......................27 East 62d Street
BISCHOFF, HENRY, JR.........19 West 96th Street
BLACK, ALEXANDER G................70 Broadway
BLUMENSTIEL, E....................320 Broadway

36

BLUMENTHAL, JOSEPH.............157 East 73d Street
BONSALL, FERDINAND..............139 Duane Street
BOOKMAN, A. L..................114 Nassau Street
BOYLE, JAMES W.................150 West 12th Street
BRIGGS, S. ELLIS...................305 Cherry Street
BRIGGS, JAMES A....................32 Nassau Street
BRITTON, GEORGE F................66 Third Avenue
BROOKS, REMSEN G...................36 New Street
BROWN, WILLIAM L....................31 Park Row
BROWN, MARTIN B..............931 Madison Avenue
BROWN, GEORGE W., JR................41 Park Row
BRUNO, RICHARD M....................146 Broadway
BUCHANAN, CHARLES P...............101 Wall Street
BUCKI, CHARLES L.............13th Street and N. R.
BUDDECKE, L. HAZARD................150 Broadway
BURDICK, F. M..................169 West 79th Street
BURNHAM, F. A...................66 East 78th Street
BURR, WILLIAM P.....................206 Broadway
BUSHE, EUGENE L.....................150 Broadway
BYRNE, JAMES........................45 William Street

C

CALHOUN, J. C........................80 Broadway
CAMPBELL, HENRY..................49 Vesey Street
CANDA, CHARLES J....................11 Pine Street

RESIDENT MEMBERS

CANTOR, JACOB A..............140 East 104th Street
CARAGHER, FRANCIS................66 Morton Street
CARDOZA, MICHAEL H................120 Broadway
CAREY, WILLIAM F.. ....61 Broadway
CARNOCHAN, G. M.................250 Fifth Avenue
CARROLL, JOHN F..............307 East 51st Street
CASEY, THOMAS B....................71 4th Avenue
CEBALLOS, JUAN M..................80 Wall Street
CHANDLER, JAMES E....................50 Broadway
CHANLER, JOHN ARMSTRONG..........Manhattan Club
CHAPIN, F. H.....................76 Leonard Street
CHARLES, R. P..............15 South William Street
CLARK, WILLIAM A....................35 Wall Street
CLARK, WILLIAM H......................2 Tryon Row
CLAUSSEN, GEORGE C........... ..170 East 73d Street
CLIFFORD, THOMAS B..................206 Broadway
CLINCHY, ANTHONY...............336 East 13th Street
COCHRAN, R. L.......................874 Broadway
COBIN, I. JONES.................166 West 54th Street
COLE, HUGH L........................59 Wall Street
COLEMAN, JAMES S.................38 East 69th Street
COLEMAN, MICHAEL...............54 West 38th Street
COMPTON, A. T.......................237 Broadway
CONKLIN, WILLIAM A.......187th Street and 10th Street
CONLON, LEWIS J...............126 East 10th Street

RESIDENT MEMBERS

CONNOLLY, J. W. . . . . 1202 Lexington Avenue
CONNOLY, THEODORE . . . . 2 Tryon Row
COOK, WILLIAM W. . . . . 15 Wall Street
COOPER, EDWARD . . . . 12 Washington Square
CORNELL, GEORGE W. . . . . 40 West 92d Street
COUDERT, FREDERIC R. . . . . 68 William Street
COWEN, ESEK . . . . 15 Wall Street
COXE, HENRY B. . . . . 3 West 30th Street
COXE, MACGRANE . . . . 51 Wall Street
CRAIN, T. C. T. . . . . 280 Broadway
CRAM, J. SERGEANT . . . . Pier A, North River
CREMIN, DR. P. W. . . . . 848 Lexington Avenue
CRIMMINS, THOMAS E. . . . . 1043 Third Avenue
CRIMMINS, JOHN D. . . . . 1043 Third Avenue
CRUIKSHANK, A. B. . . . . 135 Broadway
CUMING, P. MCGREGOR . . . . Manhattan Club
CUMISKY, EUGENE J. . . . . 727 Lexington Avenue
CURTIS, F. KINGSBURY . . . . 58 William Street
CURTIS, WILLIAM EDMOND . . . . 58 William Street
CUSKLEY, P. J. . . . . 132 East 66th Street

D

DALY, AUGUSTIN . . . . 14 West 50th Street
DALY, JOSEPH F. . . . . 19 East 62d Street
DALY, DANIEL . . . . 58 Edgecombe Avenue

RESIDENT MEMBERS

DAVIDSON, GEORGE T.....................45 Broadway
DAVIES, WILLIAM E...... ....120 Broadway
DAVIS, DANIEL A.................43 West 32d Street
DEADY, JOHN A........................59 Wall Street
DEAN, WILLIAM M..................2013 Fifth Avenue
DELANY, JOHN J..................441 West 34th Street
DESHON, CHARLES A....................237 Broadway
DESSAR, LEO C........................261 Broadway
DESSAR, DR. LEONARD A..........58 West 49th Street
DESSAU, DR. S. HENRY............47 West 56th Street
DEVEREUX, J. CLARKSON................111 Broadway
DE WITT, PETER.......................111 Broadway
DICKERSON, A. J........Storehouse, Blackwell's Island
DIETER, FREDERICK J..................35 Wall Street
DILLEY, CHARLES H.............. .140 Nassau Street
DILLON, J. RHINELANDER............59 Liberty Street
DIMOCK, HENRY F..............Pier 11, North River
DOAK, GEORGE F.........10th Avenue and 153d Street
DONNELL, EZEKIEL J....................2 Stone Street
DONOHUE, CHARLES, JR.............7 East 65th Street
DONOHUE, FRANCIS L. ....7 East 65th Street
DOSCHER, LOUIS M....................243 Broadway
DOUGHERTY, M. C.................15 West 26th Street
DOYLE, JOHN F...................125 East 70th Street
DOYLE, JOHN F., JR....... ..... .125 East 70th Street

40

DOYLE, LOUIS F..................64 St. Marks Place
DUGGETT, WILLIAM J..............66 West 53d Street
DUGRO, PHILIP H.......................Court House
DUGRO, FRANCIS A.....................36 Park Row
DUNPHY, LAWRENCE................Blackwell's Island
DUPRÉ, OVIDE.........................290 Broadway
DURYEA, CARLL S...............128 West 83d Street
DUSENBERRY, W. L.............361 Produce Exchange
DYETT, ANTHONY R...................P. O. Box 1530
DYKES, ANDREW F..............339 West 45th Street

E

EARLE, FERDINAND P...............Hotel Normandie
EHRET, FRANK A....................1197 Park Avenue
EINSTEIN, BENJAMIN F............71 East 80th Street
ELDERD, W. E.....................2281 Third Avenue
ELKUS, A. I.........................31 Nassau Street
ENGELHORN, LOUIS...................13 Cedar Street
ERNEST, JOSEPH S.......................80 Broadway
ESSON, WILLIAM...........53 South Washington Square

F

FAIRCHILD, CHARLES S.................46 Wall Street
FALK, GEORGE W..................30 West 23d Street
FANNING, WILLIAM J....................120 Broadway

RESIDENT MEMBERS

FARLEY, JAMES A................102 West 73d Street
FARLEY, JOHN T.................102 West 73d Street
FARRELL, E. D..................329 West 57th Street
FARQUHAR, PERCIVAL.............1 East 28th Street
FAY, J. ROCKWELL...............P. O. Box 3563
FEITNER, THOMAS L..............Tryon Row
FERGUS, THOMAS H...............784 Broadway
FERRIS, CHARLES W..............240 10th Avenue
FISHER, THOMAS R...............Manhattan Club
FITCH, ASHBEL P................93 Nassau Street
FITZGERALD, JAMES..............32 Chambers Street
FITZGERALD, FRANK T............200 Broadway
FLANNAGAN, W. W................80 Wall Street
FLETCHER, A. W.................761 7th Avenue
FLETCHER, J. C. C..............190 Avenue C
FLOWER, ROSWELL P..............52 Broadway
FLOWER, A. R...................52 Broadway
FORD, P. J.....................56 E. 41st Street
FOSTER, ROGER..................35 Wall Street
FOX, PATRICK...........152d Street and Hudson River
FOX, JOHN......................10 East 50th Street
FRANK, JULIUS J................62 William Street
FRANKENHEIMER, JOHN............15 Wall Street
FRESHMAN, S. D.................19 Park Place
FROST, LEANDER L...............108 West 123d Street

FRYER, WILLIAM J. .... 19 Broadway
FULLER, PAUL..................70 William Street

G

GABAY, HENRY G.................892 Third Avenue
GARDEN, HUGH R..................32 Nassau Street
GIBSON, WILLIAM J................... 120 Broadway
GILDERSLEEVE, HENRY A...............Court House
GILON, EDWARD......................11½ City Hall
GILROY, THOMAS F...............7 West 121st Street
GILROY, J. J....................... 121 Front Street
GLEASON, JOSEPH................216 East 50th Street
GODFREY, MACAULAY S............123 Front Street
GOLDBERG, SAMUEL....................Court House
GRACE, WILLIAM R.................Hanover Square
GRAHAM, JOHN C................42 Cotton Exchange
GRANT, HUGH J.................261 West 73d Street
GRAY, DR. LANDON CARTER.........6 East 49th Street
GRAYBILL, JAMES EDWARD.............229 Broadway
GREEN, GEORGE WALTON...............11 Pine Street
GREENBAUM, SAMUEL.................170 Broadway
GREENFIELD, HENRY...................35 Broadway
GREGG, JOSHUA..................1 East 14th Street
GRIFFIN, BENJAMIN..............41 West 58th Street
GROSSMAYER, E. H..................98 Bleecker Street

RESIDENT MEMBERS

GUINDON, EUGENE W................216 Duane Street
GUYTON, H. PAGE.................. 222 Fifth Avenue

H

HAGGERTY, J. H..................135 East 71st Street
HALL, CHARLES R.....Columbus Avenue and 72d Street
HALSEY, JACOB L......................156 Broadway
HALSEY, SAMUEL W................955 Sixth Avenue
HAND, CLIFFORD A....................51 Wall Street
HANFORD, SOL......................35 William Street
HARDING, GEORGE E...............40 Exchange Place
HARLAND, THOMAS..................32 Nassau Street
HARLAND, HENRY..................35 Beekman Place
HARRIS, CHARLES N...............54 William Street
HARRIS, R. DUNCAN...............20 Exchange Place
HARRIS, ROBERT L....................61 Wall Street
HARRISON, DR. GEORGE T........221 West 23d Street
HASCALL, THEODORE F.................71 Broadway
HASKINS, C. W.......................2 Nassau Street
HASTINGS, GEORGE D............50 West 9th Street
HATCH, ROSWELL D....................52 Broadway
HAULENBEEK, PETER............... 170 Duane Street
HAYES, JOHN....................217 East 50th Street
HAYES, CHARLES J..................85 Grand Street
HAYS, DANIEL P.......................170 Broadway

44

RESIDENT MEMBERS

HAYS, EUGENE D.................11 East 61st Street
HEBERT, HENRY B............110 Produce Exchange
HENDRICK, PETER A................20 Nassau Street
HENDRICKS, ARTHUR T............ ..Manhattan Club
HENRY, RICHARD M.................7 Nassau Street
HERTLE, JOHN C...............141 Washington Place
HERTS, ABE H................... ....390 Broadway
HERTS, MAURICE A............. ..242 Fifth Avenue
HERTS, JACQUES H... ....242 Fifth Avenue
HIGGINS, CECIL C.....................48 Wall Street
HILDBURGH, HENRY....................206 Broadway
HODGKINS, ARTHUR P................44 Broad Street
HOGG, CHARLES B..................124 Maiden Lane
HOLLISTER, DOUGLAS...............75 Leonard Street
HOLME, LEICESTER..... ....41 Park Row
HORNBLOWER, WILLIAM B...........45 William Street
HORWITZ, OTTO.......................280 Broadway
HOTCHKISS, HENRY D...............32 Nassau Street
HOTCHKISS, JAMES F........... ....112 Liberty Street
HOUSMAN, ARTHUR A.......... ...52 Exchange Place
HOWARD, CARLOS H...............19 William Street
HOWELL, CHARLES...............226 West 24th Street
HUBBARD, FRANK H............... ..34 Beaver Street
HUDSON, C. I..........................35 Wall Street
HUERSTEL, EDMOND....................290 Broadway

RESIDENT MEMBERS

HULME, GEORGE B.................59 Wall Street
HUNT, J. HAMILTON............245 Columbus Avenue
HUTCHINS, WALTER HILSON..........Manhattan Club
HYLAND, J. AUG.......................45 Broadway
HUSSON, DR. F. C..............12 West 39th Street

INGERSOLL, CHARLES D................170 Broadway
ISAACS, MONTEFIORE................62 New Street
ISRAEL, GEORGE M....................54 Wall Street

J

JACKSON, CHARLES A..............16 Exchange Place
JACKSON, CHARLES E............139 East 19th Street
JACOBS, ABRAHAM L................140 Nassau Street
JACOBS, E. A...................665 Madison Avenue
JACOBUS, DR. ARTHUR M.........126 West 48th Street
JANEWAY, JAMES G.................50 West 9th Street
JOHNSON, CHARLES H............103 West 55th Street
JONES, BASSETT.........................64 Broadway
JONES, CHARLES L....................67 Wall Street
JONES, SAM B..................141 West 47th Street

K

KEANE, DAVID.......................P. O. Box 2559
KEENER, WILLIAM A................Columbia College

KEITH, BOUDINOT.........................111 Broadway
KELLOGG, L. LAFLIN....................120 Broadway
KELLY, EDWARD....................45 Exchange Place
KELLY, THOMAS H..................45 Exchange Place
KENNY, WILLIAM J. K........................City Hall
KENT, ANDREW W..................17 East 57th Street
KIERNAN, ALFRED T....................170 Broadway
KIERNAN, PATRICK........44th Street and First Avenue
KILBRETH, JAMES T...............230 East 18th Street
KNUBEL, HERMAN...................82 Church Street
KOCH, JOSEPH........................54 Bond Street
KOHN, OTTO......................32 East 68th Street
KRETZER, DR. CHARLES P........124 West 41st Street
KUGELMAN, J.....................23 West 52d Street

L

LAMB, GILBERT D...................5 Beekman Street
LAMONT, DANIEL S..................35 Wall Street
LARDNER, WILLIAM J..................102 Broadway
LAROCQUE, JOSEPH....................P. O. Box 2911
LARREMORE, WILBUR...............32 Nassau Street
LEARY, WILLIAM V...............173 West 87th Street
LEAVITT, JOHN BROOKS.................111 Broadway
LEO, JOHN P.........................38 Park Row
LEVENTRITT, DAVID...................280 Broadway

RESIDENT MEMBERS

LEVY, MITCHELL A. C................89 White Street
LEVY, L. NAPOLEON.................32 Nassau Street
LEVY, JEFFERSON M................32 Nassau Street
LEVY, GEORGE W................121 West 78th Street
LEVY, JOHN J....................21 West 50th Street
LEWISOHN, JESSE................48 East 60th Street
LICHTENSTADTER, SAMUEL..........33 West 76th Street
LINSON, JOHN J......................96 Broadway
LITTLE, JOSEPH J.....................10 Astor Place
LITTLE, JOHN T., JR.............168 Pulitzer Building
LIVINGSTON, L. H....................96 Broadway
LOENING, ALBERT................82 West 68th Street
LOGAN, WALTER S...................58 William Street
LOONEY, ROBERT.....................P. O. Box 3393
LOWERRE, JAMES.................54 West 54th Street
LUMMIS, J. MAXWELL.................58 Wall Street
LYDECKER, CHARLES E.................120 Broadway
LYNN, JOHN....................141 West 11th Street
LYON, J. LEWIS.................124 West 123d Street

M

MACGREGOR, W. ALEXANDER......102 West 55th Street
MACK, HUGO S.....................5 Beekman Street
MACKELLER, THOMAS................132 Nassau Street

RESIDENT MEMBERS

MACKLIN, JOHN J.......................156 Broadway
MACLEAN, CHARLES F ....20 Nassau Street
MACRAE, WILLIAM F..................237 Broadway
MAGEE, DR. CHARLES K........1045 Lexington Avenue
MAITLAND, THOMAS A......... ....4 East 54th Street
MALCOLM, J. F....................17 East 80th Street
MANDELL, K.......................24 Howard Street
MARDEN, FRANCIS A....................239 Broadway
MARSHALL, CHARLES C ....35 William Street
MARTENS, GEORGE F...............20 Gramercy Park
MARTIN, JAMES J................ .300 Mulberry Street
MASON, ALFRED BISHOP... . .....16 West 11th Street
MAY, LEWIS.....................21 West 56th Street
MAYER, OTTO J.....................7 Bridge Street
MCADAM, DAVID.......................Court House
MCADAM, GEORGE H..............119 Nassau Street
MCCARTHY, JOHN HENRY...................City Hall
MCCORMICK, M...... ....51 Chambers Street
MCCORMICK, STEPHEN............146 East 27th Street
MCCLURE, DAVID........... ......22 William Street
MCCURDY, DELOS............... ...2 Wall Street
MCGOWAN, JOHN E...............15 West 96th Street
MCGRATH, ROBERT HUNTER, JR......32 Nassau Street
MCKEWAN, JAMES B.....:..............21 Park Row
MCMAHON, FULTON...................111 Broadway

RESIDENT MEMBERS

McMahon, Martin T. . . . . 40 Park Row
McNulty, J. R. . . . . 91 Wall Street
McNulty, G. W. . . . . 111 West 38th Street
Mead, Walter H. . . . . 65 Wall Street
Meakim, Alexander. . . . . 54 Bond Street
Messemer, Dr. Michael J. B. . . . . . 150 Second Avenue
Metzger, Otto J. . . . . 7 Maiden Lane
Michels, Jesse. . . . . 32 West 23d Street
Miller, Jacob F. . . . . 120 Broadway
Miner, Henry Clay. . . . . 115 East 34th Street
Minzesheimer, C. C. . . . . 7 Wall Street
Mitchell, William L. . . . . 110 Water Street
Monroe, Robert G. . . . . 140 Nassau Street
Montant, Jules A. . . . . 83 Worth Street
Moore, James B. . . . . 153 West 60th Street
Morgan, Rollin M. . . . . 40 Park Row
Morrison, L. W. . . . . 29 Wall Street
Moses, Moses H. 79 Vesey Street
Mosher, Joseph F. . . . . 62 Wall Street
Moynihan, A. W. . . . . 51 Chambers Street
Mulqueen, M. J. . . . . 165 Broadway
Munson, James E. . . . . P. O. Box 3722
Murray, Henry. . . . . 603 West 42d Street
Myers, Charles. . . . . 10 East 130th Street
Meyers, John G. H. . . . . 21 Park Row

RESIDENT MEMBERS

MYERS, NATHANIEL..................40 Wall Street
MYERS, THEODORE W..................280 Broadway

N

NADAL, CHARLES C.............339 Lexington Avenue
NAGLE, DR. JOHN T...............47 East 21st Street
NAUGHTON, B..................229 West 69th Street
NEALIS, JAMES J................251 East Broadway
NELSON, ABRAHAM....................261 Broadway
NEUSTADT, E. D..................Produce Exchange
NEWMAN, M. B..................6 East 62d Street
NICHOLAS, SIDNEY S...............6 East 35th Street
NICOLL, DE LANCEY...............32 Chambers Street
NIEDERSTADT, H. W. AUGUSTUS.......87 Beaver Street
NORTON, EX......................52 Exchange Place
NUNAN, DENIS.........................27 Park Row

O

O'CALLAGHAN, THOMAS, JR..............177 Broadway
O'CONNOR, NICHOLAS R..........34 West 129th Street
ODELL, HAMILTON.....................120 Broadway
O'DONOHUE, J. J................ 5 East 69th Street
O'DWYER, EDWARD F.............15 Whitehall Street
O'DWYER, WILLIAM H.................261 Broadway
O'GORMAN, JAMES A.............408 West 43d Street

51

OLCOTT, THOMAS W............169 West 130th Street
OLIPHANT, WILLIAM J..................258 Broadway
OLIVER, FRANCIS V. S.................145 Broadway
OPDYKE, WILLIAM S..................20 Nassau Street
ORR, WILLIAM C..................50 West 76th Street
ORR, ALBERT W.................127 East 27th Street
OSBORNE, JAMES W.................5 Beekman Street
OTIS, A. WALKER........................111 Broadway
OTTERBOURG, E........................280 Broadway
OUDIN, LUCIEN..........................45 Broadway
OWENS, WILLIAM F....................36 Broad Street

P

PAIGE, EDWARD W....................17 Fifth Avenue
PAINE, WILLIS S.......................50 Wall Street
PALMER, ARTHUR C....................280 Broadway
PAPE, ADOLPHUS D.....................96 Broadway
PARKER, JAMES H......................41 Wall Street
PARKER, FORREST H..............Produce Exchange
PARRIS, EDWARD L....................261 Broadway
PARRISH, SAMUEL L....................44 Broadway
PARSONS, CHARLES H..............34 East 62d Street
PATTERSON, EDWARD..............19 East 45th Street
PATTON, THOMAS........................Plaza Hotel

PEARL, W. E. . . . . 104 Broadway
PENDLETON, FRANK K. . . . . 44 Broadway
PERKINS, HOSEA B. . . . . Fort Washington
PETERS, A. W. . . . . 253 East 86th Street
PETERSON, DR. FREDERICK. . . . . . . 201 West 54th Street
PETTY, ROBERT D. . . . . 5 Beekman Street
PHILBIN, STEPHEN. . . . . 51 Chambers Street
PHILLIPS, A. L. . . . . 23 East 48th Street
PHILLIPS, ARTHUR. . . . . 66 Third Avenue
PHILLIPS, SYDNEY A. . . . . 91 Spring Street
PILSBURY, LEWIS D. . . . . Blackwell's Island
PLATZEK, M. WARLEY. . . . . 320 Broadway
PORTER, ANTHONY B. . . . . 154 Nassau Street
PORTER, HENRY H. . . . . 66 Third Avenue
POST, GEORGE A. . . . . 160 Broadway
POSTE, WILLIAM A. 11 Wall Street
POTTER, FREDERICK. . . . . 38 Park Row
POTTER, ORLANDO B. . . . . 38 Park Row
PUTZEL, GIBSON. . . . . 320 Broadway

R

RAPALLO, EDWARD S. . . . . 32 Nassau Street
RASINES, ANTONIO. 45 Pine Street
RAU, DR. LEONARD S. . . . . 72 West 55th Street

RESIDENT MEMBERS

REIFENBERG, MAX..................24 Jay Street
REILLY, JOHN.................314 East 14th Street
RENKAUFF, HENRY A................32 Warren Street
REYNOLDS, JOHN D...................45 Wall Street
RIDDEL, HENRY W......................Plaza Hotel
RIDDER, HERMAN..........................Tryon Row
RIDGWAY, CHARLES W...................45 Broadway
RIKER, RICHARD..................41 East 53d Street
RISLEY, JOHN E......................128 Broadway
ROBB, J. HAMPDEN..................23 Park Avenue
ROBBINS, EDWIN M...............27 East 44th Street
ROBERTS, DAVID H...............72 West 94th Street
ROBERTS, DR. CHARLES F.........69 East 54th Street
ROBERTSON, HENRY M..................319 Broadway
ROBINSON, E. RANDOLPH...............150 Broadway
RODMAN, ISAAC...............663 Lexington Avenue
ROESCH, GEORGE F...................34 First Avenue
ROOF, DR. STEPHEN W............223 West 23d Street
ROOME, J. V. B., JR............375 Washington Street
ROOSEVELT, FREDERICK.............583 Fifth Avenue
ROOSEVELT, ROBERT B.............33 Nassau Street
ROSENFELD, A....................18 East 64th Street
RUNYON, CHARLES G..................85 Grand Street
RYAN, LESLIE......................15 Broad Street
RYLEY, RUPERT A..................255 Fifth Avenue

S

SANDS, ANDREW H.	31 Pine Street
SANGER, ADOLPH L.	115 Broadway
SAUNDERS, HOWARD.	P. O. Box 3431
SAVAGE, W. W.	40 Wall Street
SAVIN, FRANK W.	26 New Street
SCHAEFER, EDWARD C.	51st Street and Park Avenue
SCHAEFER, EMIL.	51st Street and Park Avenue
SCHIFFER, L. G.	Cotton Exchange
SCHLESINGER, LEO.	128 East 74th Street
SCHUSTER, D. K.	280 Broadway
SCHWAB, ABRAHAM.	158 West 87th Street
SCULLY, P. J.	30 Columbia Street
SEAGER, JOHN C.	2 Stone Street
SEAGER, MARK.	2 Stone Street
SEXTON, GEORGE H.	58 William Street
SEXTON, J. B.	Court House
SEXTON, LAWRENCE E.	45 William Street
SHEEHAN, JOHN C.	249 West 23d Street
SHEEHY, EDWARD C.	66 Third Avenue
SHINDLER, JAMES.	54 West 56th Street
SHIPMAN, ANDREW J.	5 Beekman Street
SHIRLEY, WILLIAM F.	70 Broadway
SILL, JOHN T.	29 Broadway
SILLIMAN, C. A.	115 West 48th Street

RESIDENT MEMBERS

SIMMONS, DR. CHARLES E........742 Lexington Avenue
SIMMONS, J. EDWARD...............14 Nassau Street
SKIDMORE, JAMES H........Box 408, Milton-on-Hudson
SKINNER, E. V.........................353 Broadway
SLATTERY, JOHN....................368 Park Avenue
SLATTERY, VINCENT J............155 East 49th Street
SLOANE, CHARLES W.....................111 Broadway
SMITH, ADDISON..................22 West 56th Street
SMITH, E. P......................68 East 34th Street
SMITH, GEORGE W.................15 Gramercy Park
SMITH, H. W..........................11 Pine Street
SMITH, L. BAYARD.................77 William Street
SMITH, NELSON.....................97 Nassau Street
SMYTH, FREDERICK.....................38 Park Row
SOMBORN, J.......................8 East 86th Street
SOMBORN, E. K.......................67 Broad Street
SPEER, WILLIAM McMURTRIE.....224 West 59th Street
SPELLMAN, J. H......................Clarendon Hotel
SPENCER, JAMES C.................. Manhattan Club
SPEIR, GILBERT M., JR.................62 Wall Street
SPIES, FRANCIS..........................36 Broadway
SPRINGS, RICHARD A....................280 Broadway
STAPLER, HENRY B. B.............32 Chambers Street
STERN, BENJAMIN..................23 West 52d Street
STERN, JACOB.....................58 West 49th Street

STERNE, SIMON..................29 William Street
STETSON, FRANCIS L..................15 Broad Street
STETSON, GEORGE W.............26 East 45th Street
STILLINGS, WILLIAM E...............280 Broadway
STIMSON, DR. CHARLES W.........68 West 40th Street
STOKES, ANSON PHELPS................54 Wall Street
STONEBRIDGE, GEORGE H., JR.......72 East 83d Street
STORM, WALTON.......................1266 Broadway
STRAUS, OSCAR S...................42 Warren Street
STRAUSS, CHARLES.....................237 Broadway
SULZER, WILLIAM......................2 Wall Street
SUTHERLAND, JOHN L.................71 Wall Street

T

TALLMADGE, W. H..................Stamford, Conn.
TAYLOR, DOUGLAS....................8 Warren Street
TENNEY, L. S........................7 Nassau Street
THACHER, JOHN BOYD................Albany, N. Y.
THAIN, ALEXANDER.....................38 Park Row
THOMAS, EVAN.................426 Produce Exchange
THOMPSON, FERRIS S............297 Madison Avenue
THOMSON, EDWARD S.............30 East 60th Street
TIM, DAVID...................836 Lexington Avenue
TODD, ROBERT W.......................229 Broadway
TOMPKINS, HAMILTON B................229 Broadway

TOMLINSON, JOHN C....................40 Wall Street
TOWNSEND, JOHN D...............49 Chambers Street
TOWNSEND, ROBERT................32 Chambers Street
TRACY, JOHN M.....................572 Park Avenue
TRAYNOR, JAMES J................37 East 50th Street
TRUAX, CHARLES H......................Court House
TURNURE, LAWRENCE...................52 Wall Street
TURRELL, EDGAR A....................170 Broadway
TUSKA, BENJAMIN......................120 Broadway

V

VALENTINE, JOSEPH M..............97 Franklin Street
VAN GLAHN, JOHN......................96 Broadway
VAN HOESEN, JOHN W.................69 Wall Street
VAN NEST, G. WILLETT................62 Wall Street
VAN SCHAICK, JENKINS................32 Broad Street
VAN SLYCK, GEORGE W................120 Broadway
VAN VALKENBURGH, WILLIAM.......Dept. Public Parks, 64th Street and Fifth Avenue.
VAN WYCK, ROBERT A................City Hall, N. Y.
VERPLANCK, WILLIAM G..............54 William Street
VINCENT, JOHN......................32 Nassau Street
VOORHIS, CHARLES C......53 South Washington Square
VOORHIS, JOHN R........ ....300 Mulberry Street

W

WAINWRIGHT, J. H............22 West 46th Street
WAIT, FREDERICK S..................10 Wall Street
WALDSTEIN, MARTIN E..........450 Madison Avenue
WALGROVE, GEORGE W..........317 East 84th Street
WALKER, ISAAC..................14 East 40th Street
WALL, P. T..Waccubuc Hotel, Waccubuc Lakes, N. Y.
WALLACE, JAMES.................55 West 38th Street
WALLACH, LEOPOLD...................150 Broadway
WALLER, THOMAS M.............New London, Conn.
WALLIS, HAMILTON...................48 Wall Street
WALTERS, R. M..................57 University Place
WANN, WILLIAM D................9 West 30th Street
WARD, S. L. H......................65 Wall Street
WARNER, JOHN DEWITT.............52 William Street
WARREN, IRA D.......................170 Broadway
WARREN, LYMAN E....................280 Broadway
WARREN, WILLIAM R................81 Fulton Street
WATERBURY, JOHN I..................10 Wall Street
WATERBURY, NELSON J., JR..........32 Nassau Street
WATT, THOMAS L..................605 Fifth Avenue
WEBER, EDWARD... ....26 East 23d Street
WEED, JOHN W.......................7 Nassau Street
WEEKS, BARTOW S...............326 Chambers Street
WEEKS, FRANCIS H..................62 William Street

WEISNER, RICHARD E.................1 Barclay Street
WELLS, LAWRENCE..........7th Avenue and 52d Street
WELLS, WILLIAM HENRY................42 New Street
WHEELER, EVERETT P..............45 William Street
WHEELER, JOHN V................32 East 26th Street
WHITAKER, EDWARD G..............32 Nassau Street
WHITCOMB, DR. P. R............161 West 72d Street
WHITNEY, EDWARD B.................45 Cedar Street
WHITNEY, WILLIAM C..............2 West 57th Street
WHITING, JOHN B......................59 Wall Street
WICKES, THOMAS P.....................2 Wall Street
WILLCOX, HENRY C....................160 Broadway
WILLIAMS, ARTHUR D...................5 Dey Street
WILSON, R. T....................511 Fifth Avenue
WINSTON, DR. GUSTAVUS S...........32 Nassau Street
WISE, CHARLES.....................88 Reade Street
WITTENBERG, CHARLES J..................1 Broadway
WOLF, THEODOR......................81 New Street
WOOD, W. FERNANDO..............160 William Street
WOODBURY, CHARLES H...............33 Pine Street
WORMSER, A. J....................836 Fifth Avenue
WORMSER, ISIDORE, JR.............836 Fifth Avenue
WYATT, WILLIAM E...................160 Broadway
WYLIE, DR. W. GILL.............40 West 40th Street
WYNKOOP, DR. GERARDUS H........7 West 16th Street

Y

YALDEN, JAMES .... 11 Pine Street
YENNI, OSCAR................... 517 West 59th Street
YUENGLING, D. G., JR..128th St. and Amsterdam Ave.

NON-RESIDENT MEMBERS.

1892.

A

Abbett, Leon................229 Broadway.
Abbett, Leon, Jr.............229 Broadway.
Abbett, William F............229 Broadway.
Alden, Harry M...................Troy, N. Y.
Ames, Henry...........Lindell Hotel, St. Louis, Mo.
Andrews, C. S..................Danbury, Conn.
Apgar, George W................Ithaca, N. Y.
Atkins, Hiram..................Montpelier, Vt.
Atkinson, Edward........31 Milk St., Boston, Mass.
Atkinson, Henry M................Atlanta, Ga.
Atwater, Henry G.............East Orange, N. J.

B

Bailey, Edwin..................Patchogue, N. Y.
Baker, Pitt J..................Watertown, N. Y.
Barbour, Henry P.......The Spalding, Duluth, Minn.
Barrett, M. T....................Newark, N. J.
Barry, W. C...................Rochester, N. Y.
Beckwith, Charles...............Buffalo, N. Y.
Bedle, Joseph D...............Jersey City, N. J.

NON-RESIDENT MEMBERS

Beebe, George M..................Monticello, N. Y.
Bell, J. Snowden, Grant and Diamond Sts., Pittsburgh, Pa.
Benedict, E. C..................Greenwich, Conn.
Benedict, Thomas E., Office Sec. of State, Albany, N. Y.
Bergen, James J..................Somerville, N. J.
Biddle, Geo. W......505 Chestnut St., Philadelphia, Pa.
Bignon, F. G. du..................Savannah, Ga.
Blackwell, Francis O......15 Bodgen St., Boston, Mass.
Blair, Lewis H..................Richmond, Va.
Blum, Leon..................Galveston, Texas.
Bostwick, Walter B..................Bridgeport, Conn.
Bowman, Thomas..................Council Bluffs, Iowa.
Brady, Anthony N..................Albany, N. Y.
Breckinridge, Wm. C. P..................Lexington, Ky.
Bremner, Benjamin E.....58 Wabash Ave., Chicago, Ill.
Brice, Calvin S..................80 Broadway.
Briggs, David C..................Troy, N. Y.
Brister, Edwin Michael Putnam..................Newark, O.
Bromley, B. Gordon...3943 Locust St., Philadelphia, Pa.
Brown, Charles..................292 Church St.
Brown, Julius L..................Atlanta, Ga.
Brown, M..................Barnwell, S. C.
Bryan, Joseph..................Richmond, Va.
Bucher, T. Park..........1 Union Park, Boston, Mass.
Budlong, G. H..................160 5th Ave.

Bullock, A. G. . . . . Worcéster, Mass.
Burns, John B. . . . . Warren, Pa.
Burnett, Robert M. . . . . Southborough, Mass.

C

Campbell, Charles M. . . . . Denver, Col.
Campbell, James E. . . . . Columbus, O.
Carr, A. J. . . . . 1009 Lafayette Ave., Baltimore, Md.
Carr, Julian S. . . . . Durham, S. C.
Carrigan, Joseph F. . . . . Ridgewood, N. J.
Carroll, John Lee. . . . . 1710 H St., Washington, D. C.
Cartwright, Robert F. . . 769 Carroll St., Brooklyn, N. Y
Casonova, J. N. . . . . Philipsburg, Penn.
Cassidy, William R. . . . . Albany, N. Y.
Castleman, John B. . . . . Louisville, Ky.
Chamberlain, Eugene T. . . . . Albany, N. Y.
Chamberlain, George W., ... S. Newberry, Vt.
Chapman, Thomas B., 61 Woodlawn St., Hartford, Conn.
Chase, Norton. . . . . Albany, N. Y.
Chase, Samuel B. . . . . 396 Garfield Ave., Chicago, Ill.
Chipp, Howard, Jr. . . . . 183 Fair St., Kingston, N. Y.
Church, E. F. . . . . South Orange, N. J.
Clair, Francis R. . . . . College Point, N. Y.
Clarke, Gaylord B. . . . . Mobile, Ala.
Clegg, P. C. . . . . Americus, Ga.

NON-RESIDENT MEMBERS

Clement, N. H........... Court House, Brooklyn, N. Y.
Clopton, William C...................... 41 Wall St.
Cole, Lewis E........................... Carmel, N. Y.
Collins, Michael F....................... Troy, N. Y.
Collins, Patrick A...................... Boston, Mass.
Conkling, Cook...................... Rutherford, N. J.
Corbett, Frank E................... Butte City, Mont.
Coverly, William, 247 Washington Ave., Brooklyn, N. Y.
Craig, James........................ St. Joseph, Mo.
Crandall, S. Ashbel.................. Norwich, Conn.
Crosby, Dr. Dixi...................... Exeter, N. H.
Crosman, George H................... 8 Exchange Pl.
Cummins, Dr. William G...... 70 State St., Chicago, Ill.
Cutting, Walter...................... 5 West 16th St.

D

Daily, Peter............. Rogers Building, Boston, Mass.
Dambmann, C. F. W..... P. O. Box 437, Baltimore, Md.
Dannenberg, Joe........................ Macon, Ga.
Davies, L. A.,......................... Chicago, Ill.
Davis, Clinton B..................... Higgamun, Conn.
Decker, James D..................... Pond Eddy, N. Y.
Delafield, A. Floyd................... Noroton, Conn.
Denman, Frederick A. B............... Ventura, Cal.
Desmond, J. J...................... Norwich, Conn.

NON-RESIDENT MEMBERS

Devine, Thomas J..................Rochester, N. Y.
Dexter, James W........1306 Champa St., Denver, Colo.
Dickinson, Don M.....................Detroit, Mich.
Doane, J. W...........................Chicago, Ill.
Drake, George W.......................Corning, N. Y.
Driscoll, C. T......................New Haven, Conn.
Dugan, Edward G....631 Jersey Ave., Jersey City, N. J.
Duke, R. T. W., Jr................Charlottesville, Va.
Duryea, Charles T......................Babylon, N. Y.
Duryea, Stephen C. ....Babylon, N. Y.

E

Eaton, James W, Jr....................Albany, N. Y.
Edwards, Franklin............... North Wilbraham, Mass.
Edwards, William D..1 Exchange Pl., Jersey City, N. J.
Edwards, O. Wendell...............Northampton, Mass.
Eliel, Levi A..............3538 Ellis Ave., Chicago, Ill.
Ellicott, Eugene......3717 Spruce St., Philadelphia, Pa.
Ellis, Matt. H........................Yonkers, N. Y.
Elwood, S. Dow.. ....Detroit, Mich.
Ely, W. Caryl....................Niagara Falls, N. Y.
Ely, William H. H................ Tarrytown, N. Y.
Emerson, H. M... ....Wilmington, N. C.
Ensign, S. P..... ....Lime Rock, Conn.
Elting, E. J.........1301 Walnut St., Philadelphia, Pa.

NON-RESIDENT MEMBERS

Eustace, Alexander C. ....Elmira, N. Y.
Evans, Cornelius H............. .... ..Hudson, N. Y.

F

Farquhar, A. B..................... ....York, Penn.
Fearing, Daniel B.....................Newport, R. I.
Fennessy, A. L.................... ...40 Park Row.
Fields, A. C.....................Dobbs Ferry, N. Y.
Fitz-Gerald, John E........27 School St., Boston, Mass.
Folger, Henry....................... Kingston, Ont.
Foote, R. D............Lock Box 34, Morristown, N. J.
Forshay, Nelson G........... ....Peekskill, N. Y.
Frayser, R. Dudley..................Memphis, Tenn.
Freligh, Irving.....................Red Hook, N. Y.
French, Nathaniel..................Davenport, Iowa.

G

Galligher, James..................New Haven, Conn.
Gannon, William P...................Syracuse, N. Y.
Gardner, Lawrence................Washington, D. C.
Garretson, A. L........95 Mercer St., Jersey City, N. J.
Gaul, Edward L............... ....Hudson, N. Y.
Gaynor, John F.. ....Fayetteville, N. Y.
Geissenhaimer, J. A....................Freehold, N. J.
Ginter, Lewis........................Richmond, Va.

68

Gordon, Leonard J., 485 Jersey Ave., Jersey City, N. J.
Graef, Charles H..........................98 Duane St.
Graham, John.....................Mount Vernon, N. Y.
Graham, W. S. S..................Mount Vernon, N. Y.
Green, James W......................Gloversville, N. Y.
Gregory, S. S.............................Chicago, Ill.
Grice, Frank.........................San Antonio, Texas.
Griffin, Daniel G.......................Watertown, N. Y.
Griffith, Lewis E............................Troy, N. Y.
Gross, W. H.................................Lee, Mass.
Gruaz, Timothy..........................Highland, Ill.
Guggenheimer, Max......................Lynchburg, Va.

H

Haldeman, W. B..........................Louisville, Ky.
Hale, Edward J.......................Fayetteville, N. C.
Hall, Frank de P........................51 Broad Street.
Hall, George..........................Ogdensburg, N. Y.
Hall, John H..........................Hartford, Conn.
Hall, Dr. W. H........The Lakewood, Lakewood, N. J.
Halsey, L. B..............................955 6th Ave.
Hamlin, Charles S..........Kent St., Brookline, Mass.
Hanes, J. K..........59 Dearborn St., Chicago, Ill.
Hanlon, Thomas............................Helena, Mont.
Hart, Charles..........................Philadelphia, Pa.

Harter, Michael D...................... Mansfield, O.
Haselton, Seneca .... Burlington, Vt.
Hastings, Henry E......... 79 Elm St., Hartford, Conn.
Healey, Edward J................ Far Rockaway, N. Y.
Heaney, George A....... 283 Fifth St., Jersey City, N. J.
Hengerer, William..................... Buffalo, N. Y.
Heppenheimer, William C............... 229 Broadway.
Hoadly, George...................... 33 East 50th St.
Hobby, W. E........................... Holley, N. Y.
Hobson, Henry W...................... Denver, Col.
Hoffman, Albert....................... Hoboken, N. J.
Holbrook, Edwin M............. .... Albany, N. Y.
Holt, William T................ New Brighton, N. Y.
Hone, Alexander K.................. Rochester, N. Y.
Hone, John, Jr........................ 62 New Street.
Honey, Samuel R....... 12 Francis St., Newport, R. I.
Hopkins, James........................ St. Louis, Mo.
Hoyne, F. G............. 88 La Salle St., Chicago, Ill.
Hoyne, Dr. T. S....... 1833 Indiana Ave., Chicago, Ill.
Hutchinson, C. W...................... Utica, N. Y.
Hutchinson, C. H.... 1617 Walnut St., Philadelphia, Pa.
Hyatt, James W.......... .... Norwalk, Conn.
Hyde, William W..................... Hartford, Conn.

Ingalls, M. E......................... Cincinnati, O.

J

Jacobson, R. S. .... P. O. Box 724, N. Y.
Johnston, C. A. .... Birmingham, Ala.
Johnstone, W. H. .... .. Chestnut Hill, Philadelphia, Pa.
Jones, Edward F. .... Binghamton, N. Y.
Jones, Charles H. ... . St. Louis, Mo.

K

Kehrhahn, O. G. H. ...... 2 Holliday St., Baltimore, Md.
Kent, Linden. .... Washington, D. C.
Keys, William J. .... South Branch, N. J.
Kilmer, C. E. ... . 35 Seventh St., Troy, N. Y.
Kilvert, Maxwell A. .... 29 Broadway.
Kimball, W. S. .... Rochester, N. Y.
Kirchwey, G. W. .... Columbia College.
Kirtland, John C. .... East Orange, N. J.
Knapp, Charles W. ... . St. Louis, Mo.
Knapp, Robert M., Jr. .... Tarrytown, N. Y.
Knight, Herbert W. .... 233 Jackson St., Chicago, Ill.
Knox, John B. .... Anniston, Ala.
Kohn, Edwin D. .... Chicago, Ill.
Kruttschnitt, E. B. .... New Orleans, La.
Kuppenheimer, Philip, 1706 Michigan Ave., Chicago, Ill.

L

Lattamer, Emery. .... Bryan, O.
Lawson, J. A. .... 37 Maiden Lane, Albany, N. Y.

Leavitt, George O.................62 Leonard St.
Lemon, R. J........1220 Chestnut St., Philadelphia, Pa.
Levy, M. P.............Box 16, New Orleans, La.
Lewis, Thomas S..................45 William St.
Lightfoot, Alfred R................27 W. 43d St.
Lilienthal, Frederick.............Montgomery, Ala.
Lincoln, Waldo..................Worcester, Mass.
Lippincott, J. H....617 Pavonia Ave., Jersey City, N. J.
Lockwood, J. B................White Plains, N. Y.

M

Mackey, Spoor...........3860 Lake Ave., Chicago, Ill.
Mahan, Bryan F................New London, Conn.
Manning, James H..................Albany, N. Y.
Marvin, Frederick..................Detroit, Mich.
Maynard, Isaac H..................Albany, N. Y.
McCarren, P. H. ....169 Wythe Ave., Brooklyn, N. Y.
McClelland, Charles P.................40 Wall St.
McDermott, Allan L..............Jersey City, N. J.
McDonald, Samuel J......770 Broad St., Newark, N. J.
McKinney, James...............Susquehanna, N. Y.
McKinnie, William J..................Cleveland, O.
McLean, A. A.........87 Water St., Newburgh, N. Y.
McMahon, John A......................Dayton, O.
McMenamin, John F., 1200 Chestnut St., Philadelphia, Pa.
McNally, J. J...........264 Vine St., Youngstown, O.

Menken, J. Stanwood..................Memphis, Tenn.
Miller, Frank A......................Denver, Col.
Miller, Dr. George L.................Omaha, Neb.
Miller, J. B.........................Little Rock, Ark.
Miller, Joseph O.....................Mount Kisco, N. Y.
Mitchell, John L.....................Milwaukee, Wis.
Moak, Nathaniel C....... 79 Chapel St., Albany, N. Y.
Montgomery, R. E.....................Denver, Col.
Moore, Henry A..........Court House, Brooklyn, N. Y.
Morgan, Frank E......................New Haven, Conn.
Morgan, Dr. William D................Hartford, Conn.
Morrison, James F........15 South St., Baltimore, Md.
Myers, Herman........................Savannah, Ga.

N
Naphen, Henry F..........61 Court St., Boston, Mass.
Nau, Alfred E........................Pittsburg, Kansas.
Neely, William.......................New Haven, Conn.
Newell, Otis K........68 St. James Ave., Boston, Mass.
Nostrand, Warren H...................Dobbs Ferry, N. Y.
Nugent, John A.......................Middlebush, N. J.
Nunn, Dr. R. J.......................Savannah, Ga.

O
Onahan, William J......37 MacAlister Pl., Chicago, Ill.
O'Reilly, Frank C....................Orange, N. J.

P

Palmer, J. W.......... 30 Prince St., Rochester, N. Y.
Pechin, E. C........ ....Bayshore, N. Y.
Peirce, James Mills.................Cambridge, Mass.
Pell, Arthur...................Highland Falls, N. Y.
Pierce, H. C........ ....St. Louis, Mo.
Phillips, Henry, Jr...1811 Walnut St., Philadelphia, Pa.
Platt, William P................. White Plains, N. Y.
Plumer, Henry B..516 Girard Building, Philadelphia, Pa.
Plunkett, Joseph D................New Haven, Conn.
Polhemus, J. Arthur................... Nyack, N. Y.
Prather, John G........516 North Levee, St. Louis, Mo.
Price, William Henry..633 Walnut St., Philadelphia, Pa.
Prince, William A....................Southold, N. Y.
Putnam, William L.................. Portland, Me.

Q

Quincy, Josiah.........................Quincy, Mass.
Quinn, J. P..... ....Little Rock, Ark.

R

Rafferty, John P...................East Orange, N. J.
Rambant, Thomas D...270 Gates Ave., Brooklyn, N. Y.
Revere, Paul.....................Morristown, N. J.
Reynolds, George N...................Lancaster, Pa.

Richberg, J. C.... ....2335 Indiana Ave., Chicago, Ill.
Rice, William G................ ....Albany, N. Y.
Ridgway, James W.....246 Gates Ave., Brooklyn, N. Y.
Riley, John B................. ..Plattsburgh, N. Y.
Riley, Thomas............300 Bacon St., Boston, Mass.
Robertson, Alex. C..................Montville, Conn.
Robinson, George M...................Elmira, N. Y.
Robinson, Thomas H....62 South St., Morristown, N. J.
Rogers, S. B..........................60 Liberty St.
Rogers, George Mills...95 Washington St., Chicago, Ill.
Rowan, D. Noble...... ....50 Broadway.
Russell, Charles T., Jr........ ... ..Cambridge, Mass.
Russell, Henry P.... .....470 Main St., Orange, N. J.
Russell, John E.....................Leicester, Mass.
Russell, Talcott H. ...64 Grove St., New Haven, Conn.

S

Sandford, George D.....1209 Main St., Peekskill, N. Y.
Schwarzwaelder, William............ ....37 Fulton St.
Schwerd, J....................... ...Anniston, Ala.
Scott, Frederick R....................Richmond, Va.
Sears, John G.........................Owego, N. Y.
Seward, George F.................East Orange, N. J.
Seymour, Charles J.... ....Brookline, Mass.
Sheehan, William F....................Buffalo, N. Y.

NON-RESIDENT MEMBERS

Shepard, C. D.................................84 W. 120th St.
Sherman, Frank E.....................Jamestown, N. Y.
Slattery, E. J............................Albany, N. Y.
Smalley, B. B..........................Burlington, Vt.
Smith, A. B............................38 Park Row.
Smith, Bolton.........................Memphis, Tenn.
Smith, Robert J.........160 La Salle St., Chicago, Ill.
Smyth, Albert H.......126 S. 22d St., Philadelphia, Pa.
Soper, Royal R........................Elmira, N. Y.
Sproat, Charles L......................55 Liberty St.
Stark, Benjamin....................New London, Conn.
Stark, William M...................New London, Conn.
Steel, W. J..........................Memphis, Tenn.
Stewart, Shellman B.....................83 Worth St.
Stillwell, Wellington..................Millersburg, O.
Stoever, Charles M......520 Minor St., Philadelphia, Pa.
Stratton, Charles E....................Boston, Mass.
Streeter, Frederick..................Watertown, N. Y.
Swan, Alden S., 189 Columbia Heights, Brooklyn, N. Y.
Sweeny, William H....................Yonkers, N. Y.

T

Tabor, Charles F......................Albany, N. Y.
Taggart, M. W........................Pine Bluff, Ark.
Tappin, Henry A........................80 South St.

Tate, Alfred O.................................Orange, N. J.
Taylor, J. Henry......... .82 Water St., Boston, Mass.
Taylor, S. S...............................Elmira, N. Y.
Taylor, W. H............................Stamford, Conn.
Ten Eyck, Dr. J. A....................Bridgeport, Conn.
Thatcher, H. C....................Yarmouth Port, Mass.
Thompson, Robert Hallam.................Troy, N. Y.
Thurman, Allen W.......................Columbus, O.
Tillinghast, Philip.... ....Moscow, Idaho.
Tracey, Charles..........................Albany, N. Y.
Troup, Alexander.....................New Haven, Conn.
Truman, James C..................Binghamton, N. Y.

V

Van Buren, Augustus.................Kingston, N. Y.
Vanhorne, D. A............25 Main St., Orange, N. J.
Van Vleet, De Forest...................Ithaca, N. Y.
Van Wyck, Augustin, 172 Hancock St., Brooklyn, N. Y.
Van Wyck, William...172 Hancock St., Brooklyn, N. Y.
Vroom, James W...........................Denver, Col.

W

Wadley, H. G..........................Wytheville, Va.
Wadsworth, Charles F................Genesee, N. Y.
Walsh, Denis T........................Ansonia, Conn.
Wandell, Charles B.....................96 Fifth Ave.

NON-RESIDENT MEMBERS

Ward, Charles A..................Port Huron, Mich.
Watson, Thomas T............. ...Morristown, N. J.
Watson, William L,...............Produce Exchange.
Welch, Andrew................. ....Aurora, Ill.
Weller, Augustus N....................99 Nassau St.
Wemple, Edward......................Albany, N. Y.
Werts, George T....80 Crescent Ave., Jersey City, N. J.
Wetmore, H. S........................Euclid, O.
Wheeler, George W.................Bridgeport, Conn.
White, John...........11 Yarmouth St., Boston, Mass.
Williams, M. Parker............... ....Hudson, N. Y.
Williams, Paul F....Whitehaven, New Brunswick, N. J.
Wilson, Albert A........2000 G St., Washington, D. C.
Wilson, William R...................Elizabeth, N. J.
Wittman, Caspar, Jr...................Buffalo, N. Y.
Woodbury, Gordon................Manchester, N. H.
Woodbury, Horace S................... ..1 State St.
Woodruff, William V.................Hartford, Conn.
Woolworth, J. M.....................Omaha, Neb.
Wortham, Charles E., Jr.. ....Richmond, Va.
Wright, William R..................Germantown, Pa.
Wren, P. W......................Bridgeport, Conn.

Y

Young, E. F. C....................Jersey City, N. J.

DECEASED MEMBERS

Dr. William F. Duncan.

Samuel Jones.

John Lowe.

Jerome Ottenheimer.

Percey Rockwell,

William H. Turrell.

John G. Warwick.

Lightning Source UK Ltd.
Milton Keynes UK
UKHW022116221218
334174UK00027B/2028/P